Maddie's Life Jacket

By Julie Haydon

Illustrations by
Bettina Guthridge

Contents

Capsized

One weekend, Maddie and her dad went kayaking on a river near their home. Maddie's dad carried their kayak to the river's edge. He put the kayak down and handed Maddie her helmet and a life jacket.

"Oh, no!" Maddie cried. "This is too big for me. It's Mum's life jacket." She shrugged. "It doesn't matter," she said. "I don't really need to wear one."

"Yes, you do," her dad said, sternly. "We'll go back to the car and get yours. You need to wear a life jacket that fits properly."

Ten minutes later, Maddie and her dad paddled off in their kayak. It was very peaceful on the river, and they chatted happily.

All of a sudden, two boys in their kayak came around a bend towards them. They were going very fast. Maddie's dad yelled at the boys to slow down, but it was too late. The boys' kayak hit them and they capsized.

Maddie gasped as she fell into the cold water.

She bobbed about in the water like a cork.

"Try to swim to the bank," her dad called. "I'll be right behind you. Your life jacket will keep you afloat."

Maddie started to swim. She was surprised how heavy her wet clothes felt. When she reached the bank, her dad helped her climb out of the river.

The two boys rescued the kayak and paddles and brought them to the river's edge.

Maddie's dad pulled the kayak up onto the bank.

"Sorry," the boys called out, before paddling on.

"I'm glad I wore my life jacket," Maddie said, giving her dad a big hug.

Saved by My Life Jacket

Yesterday afternoon, I went kayaking with Dad on the river.

Dad put the paddles, our helmets and the life jackets inside the kayak. He carried the kayak from the car down to the river bank.

When Dad gave me a life jacket to wear, we realised he'd brought Mum's instead of mine! I said I didn't need to wear a life jacket, but Dad said I had to wear one. So we went back to the car and got mine.

While we were paddling on the river, another kayak came around a bend very fast and hit our kayak. Dad and I fell into the river. Luckily my life jacket made it easy to stay afloat.

My wet clothes were very heavy and the deep water was very cold. If I hadn't been wearing my life jacket, it would have been really hard to swim to the bank. When I reached the bank, Dad helped me climb out of the river.

After that, the two boys who hit us got our kayak and paddles, and brought them over to us.

They were very sorry about what had happened.

It was still a fun day, even though we fell into the water. I'm glad I was wearing my life jacket!

Maddie Ellis
Aged 9 years